CONNECT THE THOTS

BIBLE TRIVIA
CHALLENGE ——→

CONNECT THE THOTS

How Are These Clues Related?

PAUL KENT

BARBOUR
PUBLISHING

ISBN 1-59310-689-0

Published by Barbour Publishing, Inc., P.O. Box 719,
Uhrichsville, Ohio 44683, www.barbourbooks.com

*Our mission is to publish and distribute inspirational products
offering exceptional value and biblical encouragement to the masses.*

 Member of the
Evangelical Christian
Publishers Association

Printed in the United States of America.
5 4 3 2 1

To the
Growing Together
Sunday school class
at Dover Bible—
Carole and Robert,
Joanne and Mike,
Kristi and Jim,
Kathy, Edward, Mike, et al.—
for whom I try to "connect the thots"
each week.

INTRODUCTION

We all make connections, every day. . .on the Internet, at the airport, with our friends. But are you ready to connect the thots?

Welcome to *Bible Trivia Challenge: Connect the Thots*, where your success is based on your skill of deduction as much as it is your knowledge of scripture.

Here's a sneak preview: fifty-two quizzes designed to plumb the depths of your Bible knowledge. . . ten questions in each quiz, with each one increasingly, perhaps even maddeningly, more difficult. . .more than five hundred questions in all, with a mind-boggling total of 286,000 points for a perfect score!

Connect the Thots is all about determining the common thread that binds three seemingly unrelated clues. For example, what one idea ties together *baby in a manger, death on a cross,* and *King of Kings*? Easy enough, right? Connect the thots with the answer Jesus. But you'll need to be pretty sharp to connect *Morasthite, a vision of Samaria and Jerusalem,* and *do justly, love mercy, and walk humbly with the Lord.* Did you figure out that they all relate to the prophet Micah? If you're up to the challenge, read on for hours of mind-bending fun!

Each question is worth from 100 to 1,000 points, with a perfect score, per quiz, of 5,500 points. Keep score as you go by entering your totals in the spaces provided following the quizzes. Answers to all *Connect the Thots* quizzes follow the final quiz and include the appropriate scripture citations. All scripture references, as well as any explanatory notes, are from the King James Version of the Bible.

Make a connection with fun as you *Connect the Thots*!

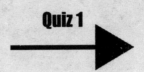

1
100 Pts

a mount
groves
Noah's dove

2
200 Pts

Daniel's "weeks"
the "other" disciples
forgiveness times seven

3
300 Pts

the Shunammite's son
Eutychus
Lazarus

 4
400 Pts

Pentecost
Jesus walks on water
Job's children

 5
500 Pts

Joseph
the ancient Israelites
Onesimus

6
600 Pts

churches of Revelation
the first deacons
clean animals on the ark

7
700 Pts

Aaron
Gershom
Miriam

8
800 Pts

Naaman
Joab
Barak

9
900 Pts

Tobiah
Ezra
King Artaxerxes

10
1000 Pts

a fire
an unruly evil
a world of iniquity

Answers on page 221.

Your Score for This Quiz: ___

12

Quiz 2

1
100 Pts

a net
a pearl
a mustard seed

2
200 Pts

Jesus' disciples
tribes of Israel
gates of the new Jerusalem

an apostle
a tanner
a sorcerer

the father of lies
the accuser of the brethren
Beelzebub

Samson
Deborah
Ehud

6
600 Pts

**Mordecai
Queen Vashti
Haman**

 7
700 Pts

**the Philippian jail
Jesus' tomb
Mt. Sinai**

 8
800 Pts

**King Solomon
Agur the son of Jakeh
King Lemuel**

9
900 Pts

Saul and Abner
Mordecai and Esther
Mary and Elizabeth

10
1000 Pts

Demetrius
Huram-Abi
Tubal-Cain

Answers on pages 221–222.

Your Score for This Quiz: ____
Running Total: ____

Quiz 3

1
100 Pts

wife of Cleophas
sister of Lazarus
mother of Jesus

2
200 Pts

fig leaves
a curse
dust

3
300 Pts

King Ahasuerus's scepter
a calf-shaped idol
the streets of the new Jerusalem

4
400 Pts

Jacob's service for Rachel
loaves to feed four thousand
Naaman at the Jordan

5
500 Pts

Diana
Baalim
Dagon

6
600 Pts

**Chilion and Orpah
Ananias and Sapphira
Isaac and Rebekah**

7
700 Pts

**Haman
Judas Iscariot
Pharaoh's chief baker**

8
800 Pts

**Babel
Siloam
Jerusalem**

9
900 Pts

the Holy Spirit
the four horsemen of Revelation
Daniel's book

10
1000 Pts

grass
a fig tree
a man's hand

Answers on pages 222–223.

Your Score for This Quiz: ____
Running Total: ____

Quiz 4

1
100 Pts

**turn stones into bread
jump from the top of the temple
worship the devil**

2
200 Pts

**Nebo
Ararat
Sinai**

3
300 Pts

**David and Eliab
Jacob and Esau
James and John**

4
400 Pts

**spying in Canaan
the sun stands still
Jericho's walls fall**

5
500 Pts

**Esther
Jezebel
Athaliah**

6
600 Pts

"your loins girt about with truth"
"the shield of faith"
"the helmet of salvation"

7
700 Pts

gold
brass
iron mixed with clay

8
800 Pts

Nicodemus and Jesus
an angel and shepherds
two angels and Lot

9
900 Pts

the rock at Horeb
the throne of God
Isaac's well

10
1000 Pts

Saul
Og
Agrippa

Answers on page 223.

Your Score for This Quiz: ____
Running Total: ____

Quiz 5 ➡

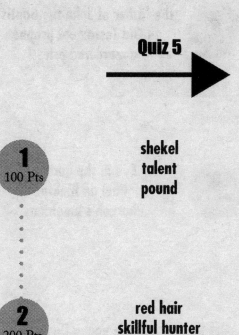

1
100 Pts

shekel
talent
pound

2
200 Pts

red hair
skillful hunter
lost birthright

**the father of John the Baptist
an Old Testament prophet
a murdered priest**

**Eve in the garden
Paul on Melita
Pharaoh's magicians**

**the young David
the prophet Amos
Jesus Christ**

6
600 Pts

**Rahab
Gomer
the woman on the beast**

7
700 Pts

**Adam's curse
Paul's ailment
Jesus' crown**

8
800 Pts

**King Uzziah
Miriam
Naaman**

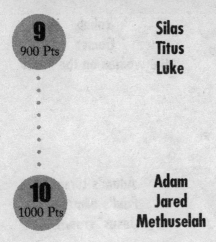

9
900 Pts

Silas
Titus
Luke

10
1000 Pts

Adam
Jared
Methuselah

Answers on pages 223–224.

Your Score for This Quiz: ____
Running Total: ____

Quiz 6

1
100 Pts

a baptizer
a son of Zebedee
surnamed Mark

2
200 Pts

a golden idol
the prodigal's party
lying with a lion

3
300 Pts

a donkey's jawbone
a riddle
a prostitute

4
400 Pts

Egypt
Capernaum
Nazareth

5
500 Pts

a lake
an offering
Moses' bush

6
600 Pts

**King Saul and David
a Roman soldier at the crucifixion
pruning hooks**

7
700 Pts

**James
Simon
Judas**

8
800 Pts

**Pharpar
Pison
Jordan**

9
900 Pts

a voice in the night
a voice for God
a voice from the grave

10
1000 Pts

Paul and Silas in prison

Jesus and His disciples on the night of His arrest

Moses and the Israelites after crossing the Red Sea

Answers on pages 224–225.

Your Score for This Quiz: ____
Running Total: ____

Quiz 7

1
100 Pts

a dove
a rainbow
the mountains of Ararat

2
200 Pts

missionary companion
of the apostle Paul

correspondent with Theophilus

beloved physician

3 300 Pts

at Cana in Galilee
of the Lamb
Jesus' parable of a king
and his son

4 400 Pts

when Rebekah met Isaac
straining out gnats
the eye of a needle

5 500 Pts

Goliath and Lahmi
Huz and Buz
Peter and Andrew

6
600 Pts

Philippi
purple cloth
convert of Paul

7
700 Pts

Bartimaeus
Peter's mother-in-law
Jairus's daughter

8
800 Pts

Jesus
the sons of Jair
Balaam

King David
Moses
Asaph

a sin of David
a duty of Moses
a command of Caesar Augustus

Answers on page 225.

Your Score for This Quiz: ____
Running Total: ____

Quiz 8

1
100 Pts

myrrh
frankincense
gold

2
200 Pts

a worm-eaten plant
an unusual fish
a sinful city of 120,000

3
300 Pts

Matthew
Zacchaeus
the man who said, "God be
merciful to me a sinner"

4
400 Pts

a bath
Solomon
Uriah the Hittite

5
500 Pts

John the Baptist
James, brother of the apostle John
Stephen

6
600 Pts

Pharaoh's cup
birds
baskets of bread

7
700 Pts

Jezebel
Elymas
a woman of Endor

8
800 Pts

gates of the holy city
parable of a merchant
swine

9
900 Pts

the false god Dagon
Satan
Jericho's walls

10
1000 Pts

Jesus
Hannah
the disciples at Pentecost

Answers on pages 225–226.

**Your Score for This Quiz: ____
Running Total: ____**

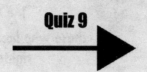

Quiz 9

1
100 Pts

shepherd

green pastures

a table "in the presence
of mine enemies"

2
200 Pts

locusts
camel's hair
wild honey

3
300 Pts

the meek
the merciful
those who hunger and thirst for righteousness

4
400 Pts

Cain
Barabbas
the devil

5
500 Pts

a sea
seasoning for speech
Lot's wife

6
600 Pts

Boaz
Obed
Jesse

7
700 Pts

merry
deceitful
hardened

8
800 Pts

a woman at a well
one thankful leper of ten cleansed
the hero of a neighborly parable

9
900 Pts

Job
Publius's father
Peter's mother-in-law

10
1000 Pts

Abinadab
Abel
Jacob

Answers on pages 226–227.

Your Score for This Quiz: ____
Running Total: ____

Quiz 10

1
100 Pts

a nap at prayer time
a miraculous catch of fish
a cock's crowing

2
200 Pts

a favored son
a dream of supremacy
a coat of many colors

3
300 Pts

"I thirst"
"Father, forgive them"
"Why hast thou forsaken me?"

4
400 Pts

a widow at Zarephath
ravens that carry food
450 prophets of Baal

5
500 Pts

Zebedee and James
David and Adonijah
Abram and Ishmael

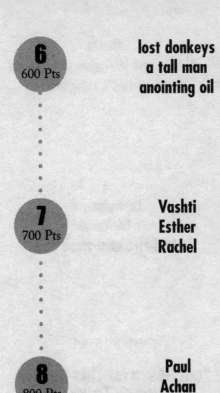

6
600 Pts

lost donkeys
a tall man
anointing oil

7
700 Pts

Vashti
Esther
Rachel

8
800 Pts

Paul
Achan
Stephen

**David
Miriam and the women of Israel
Herodias's daughter**

**Lo-Ruhamah
Lo-Ammi
Maher-Shalal-Hash-Baz**

Answers on page 227.

**Your Score for This Quiz: ____
Running Total: ____**

Quiz 11

1
100 Pts

**the Bread of Life
the True Vine
Alpha and Omega**

2
200 Pts

**honor your father and mother
don't murder
don't covet**

3
300 Pts

**Tarshish
Joppa
Nineveh**

4
400 Pts

a brother of Jesus

**the Cyrenian who carried
Jesus' cross**

a Canaanite disciple

5
500 Pts

**the serpent in the garden
a burning bush
Balaam's donkey**

6
600 Pts

four men and a crippled friend
King David, lusting for Bathsheba
Peter and his vision of
animals in a sheet

7
700 Pts

the selection of Matthias
as an apostle
soldiers competing for the crucified
Jesus' clothing
Jonah determined as the cause of
a storm at sea

8
800 Pts

John the Baptist's food
Samson's riddle
the Promised Land

9
900 Pts

**Eliphaz
Zophar
Elihu**

10
1000 Pts

**Elijah's final day
God's answer to Job
sowing the wind**

Answers on pages 227–228.

**Your Score for This Quiz: _____
Running Total: _____**

Quiz 12

1
100 Pts

Abigail and Zeruiah
Mary and Martha
Rachel and Leah

2
200 Pts

Tiberius
Claudius
Augustus

fire at Pentecost
speech to be interpreted
something no man can tame

shepherd
younger brother
murder victim

Tarsus
Lydia
the road to Damascus

6
600 Pts

the wise men and Jesus
Wormwood
the fourth day of creation

7
700 Pts

Naaman at the Jordan River
Pontius Pilate's hands
Jesus and the disciples' feet

8
800 Pts

the sons of Anak
Ishbi-Benob
Goliath

camel
vulture
pig

 a slave and an awl
false teachers and things that itch
Peter and Malchus

Answers on page 228.

Your Score for This Quiz: ___
Running Total: ___

Quiz 13

1
100 Pts

**Aceldama
a kiss
thirty pieces of silver**

2
200 Pts

**a wedding surprise
a stolen blessing
a ladder to heaven**

3
300 Pts

a vision of a ram and a goat
handwriting on a wall
a fiery furnace

4
400 Pts

the prodigal son
Legion
casting pearls

5
500 Pts

a son of Jacob
a devout man who blessed
the baby Jesus

a man also called "Niger"

6
600 Pts

**Mahlon
Elimelech
Naomi**

7
700 Pts

**Anna at the temple

a small offering commended
by Jesus

the parable of an unjust judge**

8
800 Pts

**Joseph in Egypt
Cyrenius in Syria
Pontius Pilate in Judea**

9
900 Pts

**bread upon waters
a time for everything
vanity of vanities**

10
1000 Pts

**saying, "There is no God"
despising a father's instruction
trusting in one's self**

Answers on page 229.

**Your Score for This Quiz: ____
Running Total: ____**

Quiz 14

1
100 Pts

our Father
our debts
our daily bread

2
200 Pts

James the son of Alphaeus
Thaddaeus
Bartholomew

3
300 Pts

Saul on the road to Damascus
men of Sodom, at Lot's house
Bartimaeus

4
400 Pts

Jesus' triumphal entry
Saul's mission from his dad
Balaam's interrupted journey

5
500 Pts

don't drink wine
don't cut your hair
don't touch the dead

6
600 Pts

**Unleavened Bread
Weeks
Tabernacles**

7
700 Pts

**Nadab and Abihu
Uzzah
Ananias and Sapphira**

8
800 Pts

**Miriam
Anna
Huldah**

the murdered Naboth
Jesus' parable of hired workers
Noah's drunkenness

Joseph from Cyprus
an argument with Paul
regarded as a god

Answers on pages 229–230.

Your Score for This Quiz: ___
Running Total: ___

Quiz 15

1
100 Pts

a post-flood migration
a confusion of languages
a tower to heaven

2
200 Pts

baby Moses in his floating basket
Jesus at Lazarus's tomb
Peter after denying Christ

3
300 Pts

Mary Magdalene
a fortune-telling servant girl
"Legion"

4
400 Pts

Jair's sons
Jesus' age of ministry
Judas's pieces of silver

5
500 Pts

Agabus
Habakkuk
Nathan

glorified God at the crucifixion
Cornelius of the Italian band
Jesus healed his servant

Absalom
Samson
Mary, sister of Martha

an axhead that floated
bears that mauled mouthy kids
a Shunammite boy
raised from the dead

9
900 Pts

Jesus
John the Baptist
Samson

10
1000 Pts

King Zimri
King Saul
Judas Iscariot

Answers on page 230.

Your Score for This Quiz: ___
Running Total: ___

 **Quiz 16**

1
100 Pts

shepherd
harpist
king

2
200 Pts

Elizabeth
Herod the tetrarch
a voice in the wilderness

3
300 Pts

an Ethiopian eunuch
Lydia of Thyatira
Jesus

4
400 Pts

promised
flowing with milk and honey
of Goshen

5
500 Pts

Sarai
Rachel
the wife of Manoah

6
600 Pts

the dream of Pharaoh's baker

leftovers at the feeding of
the five thousand

the apostle Paul's escape
from Damascus

7
700 Pts

Samson
Jonathan
John the Baptist

8
800 Pts

Elisha
the eagle
forbidden for priests

9
900 Pts

David spares King Saul's life

Obadiah hides
one hundred prophets of God

Lazarus is raised to life

10
1000 Pts

Elijah fleeing from Jezebel

Jonah after Nineveh's repentance

Moses when the Israelites
complained about manna

Answers on page 231.

Your Score for This Quiz: ____
Running Total: ____

Quiz 17

1
100 Pts

a woman named Zipporah
a forty-year journey
a tablet of stone

2
200 Pts

son of Saul
warrior of Israel
friend of David

3
300 Pts

a wedding in Cana
King Ahaseurus's seven-day feast
Noah's tent

 4
400 Pts

Jesus' sweat on
the Mount of Olives

the life of the flesh

robes washed white
before God's throne

5
500 Pts

Ahinoam
Abigail
Michal

a rich man's request from hell
Moses' "slowness"
speech at Pentecost

 Ananias
Caiaphas
Jesus Christ

 God has none in
the death of the wicked
of sin, for a season
at God's right hand forevermore

**Pharaoh's lost in the Red Sea
Solomon's fourteen hundred
Elijah's fiery ride into heaven**

**Jesus' mockery
Mordecai's honor
Lydia's business**

Answers on pages 231–232.

Your Score for This Quiz: ____
Running Total: ____

Quiz 18

1
100 Pts

Ham
Japheth
Shem

2
200 Pts

a place called Haran
a woman named Sarai
a command to move

3
300 Pts

a valley full of bones
a man with a measuring reed
a wheel inside a wheel

 4
400 Pts

son of Nun
successor of Moses
leader of Israel

 5
500 Pts

Bathsheba
Abigail
Anna

6
600 Pts

"I am escaped with
the skin of my teeth"

"The LORD gave,
and the LORD hath taken away"

"Naked came I out of my mother's
womb, and naked shall I return thither"

7
700 Pts

a drinking party
handwriting on a wall
knocking knees

8
800 Pts

cucumbers
melons
leeks

900 Pts

Herod of Galilee
Philip of Ituraea
Lysanias of Abilene

1000 Pts

Abib
Adar
Elul

Answers on page 232.

Your Score for This Quiz: ____
Running Total: ____

Quiz 19

1
100 Pts

the creation
the fall of man
the calling of Abraham

2
200 Pts

a cheated brother
a wrestling match
a powerful son

3
300 Pts

**two mites
two pigeons
five loaves and two fish**

4
400 Pts

**Moses and Aaron
a hard heart
plagues on Egypt**

5
500 Pts

**sin
trespass
burnt**

6
600 Pts

Legion's abode
Joseph of Arimathaea's gift to Jesus
Jesus' mocking criticism
of the Pharisees

7
700 Pts

Nimrod the builder
120,000 people
Jonah's destination

8
800 Pts

Boanerges
the giving of the Ten Commandments
the seventh plague on Egypt

9
900 Pts

a Tishbite
a three-year drought
a still small voice

10
1000 Pts

Fair Havens
Syracuse
Three Taverns

Answers on page 233.

Your Score for This Quiz: ____
Running Total: ____

Quiz 20

1
100 Pts

a carpenter
a ruler of Egypt
a rich disciple from Arimathaea

2
200 Pts

the rainfall of Noah's flood
Jesus' fast in the wilderness
Jesus' post-resurrection appearances

the twelve apostles
the sound of violent wind
other languages

your parents
better than sacrifice
God rather than men

Ezra's devotion
approved, not ashamed
the Bereans

6
600 Pts

Samson's snack of honey
David's dangerous shepherd duty
Jesus' title "of the tribe of Judah"

7
700 Pts

wild goat
leviathan
behemoth

8
800 Pts

he lied to the apostles
he restored Saul's sight
he ordered the apostle Paul struck

Memucan
Hegai
Bigthan

handkerchiefs
aprons
a shadow

Answers on pages 233–234.

Your Score for This Quiz: ___
Running Total: ___

Quiz 21

1
100 Pts

the meek
the poor in spirit
the peacemakers

2
200 Pts

a spy
a companion of Caleb
"Be thou strong
and very courageous"

3
300 Pts

sons of Noah
Peter's denial of Jesus
the sign of Jonah

 4
400 Pts

a six-month party
a hanging
a celebration called Purim

 5
500 Pts

Michal
Samuel
the witch of Endor

**Paul's other occupation
the ancient tabernacle
Sisera's assassination**

**adulterers
extortioners
drunkards**

**the serpent
the day of Job's birth
anyone who hangs on a tree**

9
900 Pts

death
an adder
the locusts of Revelation

10
1000 Pts

"son of man"
eating a scroll
a watchman to the house of Israel

Answers on page 234.

Your Score for This Quiz: ___
Running Total: ___

Quiz 22

1
100 Pts

**an uncircumcised Philistine
a stone in a sling
a severed head**

2
200 Pts

**a winepress
the angel of the Lord
a fleece**

a kiss
scriptures
Ghost

three widows
gleaning barley
an unwilling kinsman

a closet
Gethsemane
inside a fish

6
600 Pts

Elkanah
Hannah
Eli the priest

7
700 Pts

God's covenant with Abraham
the eighth day
treacherous vengeance
on the Shechemites

8
800 Pts

Seleucia
Cyprus
Salamis

9
900 Pts

God's foolishness
better than rubies
Solomon's request

10
1000 Pts

the earth, to God
enemies, to Christ
a place of dishonor, to the poor

Answers on page 235.

Your Score for This Quiz: ____
Running Total: ____

Quiz 23

1
100 Pts

**Word of God
Lamb of God
Son of God**

2
200 Pts

**an abundance of frogs
three days of darkness
the death of firstborn sons**

3
300 Pts

a lamb
unleavened bread
blood on the door frames

4
400 Pts

Amos's vision of a basket

love, joy, peace, etc.

the tree of the knowledge
of good and evil

5
500 Pts

"Thy hair is as a flock of goats"

"Thy navel is like a round goblet"

"Thy nose is as the tower of
Lebanon"

Jubal
the young David
four beasts and twenty-four elders
around God's throne

Jesus' parable of ten virgins
Samuel and the young shepherd David
the widow of Zarephath

leprosy
a timbrel
Moses and Aaron

9
900 Pts

the prophet Daniel
the priest Zechariah
the virgin Mary

10
1000 Pts

Abimelech's demise
forbidden as pledge for a debt
causing a child to sin

Answers on pages 235–236.

Your Score for This Quiz: ____
Running Total: ____

Quiz 24

1
100 Pts

a persecutor
the road to Damascus
a thorn in the flesh

2
200 Pts

a house built on rock
new wine in old bottles
an unmerciful servant

the Sea of Galilee
a fisherman
the brother of Peter

Ephesus
Smyrna
Thyatira

a young protégé
wicked sons
a broken neck

6
600 Pts

Solomon's concubines
Gideon's army for fighting Midian
Enoch's years after
Methuselah's birth

7
700 Pts

one of the Seven
a talk with an Ethiopian eunuch
four unmarried daughters
who prophesied

8
800 Pts

Arcturus (the Bear)
Orion
Pleiades

9
900 Pts

a cloke (cloak)
books
parchments

10
1000 Pts

Samuel
Jesus
Josiah

Answers on page 236.

Your Score for This Quiz: ___
Running Total: ___

Quiz 25

1
100 Pts

the Transfiguration
forty years in the wilderness
the Ten Commandments

2
200 Pts

a boat
fishing nets
a man named Zebedee

3
300 Pts

carnal mindedness
"the house appointed for all living"
the wages of sin

4
400 Pts

Pergamos
Sardis
Philadelphia

5
500 Pts

shipwrecks
stoning
hunger and thirst

6
600 Pts

moths
rust
thieves

7
700 Pts

a man called Jerub-Baal
a choice army of three hundred
a dream of battling bread

8
800 Pts

Aristarchus
Tychicus
Aquila and Priscilla

9
900 Pts

meat sacrificed to idols

all appearance of evil

"fleshly lusts,
which war against the soul"

10
1000 Pts

you'll be proven a liar

you'll receive plagues

you'll lose your part
in the book of life

Answers on page 237.

Your Score for This Quiz: ____
Running Total: ____

Quiz 26

1
100 Pts

for the baby Moses
of the Covenant
Noah's

2
200 Pts

Ashpenaz
Shadrach
Abednego

a barren fig tree
a lost coin
sheep and goats

the fourth commandment
the seventh day
rest

Horeb
Gilboa
Gerizim

**father of Obed
great-grandfather of King David
husband of Ruth**

**Jesus' final Passover
the Transfiguration
Jesus' baptism**

**the seventh commandment
a lustful look
divorcing to remarry**

9
900 Pts

Jesus' parable of vinedressers
Gideon threshing wheat
a place of God's wrath

10
1000 Pts

food cooked over manure
human hair weighed in a balance
lying down for 390 days

Answers on pages 237–238.

Your Score for This Quiz: ____
Running Total: ____

Quiz 27

1
100 Pts

Seth
the garden of Eden
disobedience to God

2
200 Pts

an early inheritance
riotous living
friendlessness and starvation

3
300 Pts

a wife named Keturah
a son named Ishmael
a covenant with God

4
400 Pts

cousin of Barnabas
profitable to Paul's ministry
author of a Gospel

5
500 Pts

the darts of the wicked
the Christian's trials
Nebuchadnezzar's furnace

6
600 Pts

Jedidiah
a fleet of ships
"Divide the living child in two"

7
700 Pts

sheaves of grain
sun, moon, and eleven stars
bowing in worship

8
800 Pts

Hagar
banishment to the wilderness
"a wild man"

9
900 Pts

husband of one wife
grave
not given to much wine

10
1000 Pts

King Eglon of Moab
King Joash of Judah
King Sennacherib of Assyria

Answers on page 238.

Your Score for This Quiz: ____
Running Total: ____

Quiz 28

1
100 Pts

three sons
two of every animal
one big boat

2
200 Pts

the feeding of five thousand
the healing of Jairus's daughter
an unexpected catch of fish

3
300 Pts

Moses' spokesman
a rod that became a snake
the golden calf

4
400 Pts

longsuffering
gentleness
goodness

5
500 Pts

Isaac's question to Abraham
a story of the prophet Nathan
Jesus Christ

Aaron's budded
correction for a child
Jesus' future rule of iron

Jonah's plant
Herod's death
hell's immortal creatures

scribes and Pharisees
blind guides
Chorazin and Bethsaida

9
900 Pts

a pilgrimage
vain
a vapour

10
1000 Pts

locusts
the valley of decision
young men seeing visions

Answers on page 239.

Your Score for This Quiz: ___
Running Total: ___

120

Quiz 29

1
100 Pts

**two fish
five loaves
twelve baskets of leftovers**

2
200 Pts

**fewer than ten righteous people
raining brimstone
Gomorrah**

3
300 Pts

Moses and Aaron
Joseph and Benjamin
Cain and Abel

4
400 Pts

tree of
crown of
book of

5
500 Pts

Jacob and Rachel, upon meeting
Jonathan and David, upon parting
Judas and Jesus, at the betrayal

6
600 Pts

grievous sores on men
a bloody sea
a scorching sun

7
700 Pts

"She is not dead, but sleepeth"

elderly parents-to-be
Abraham and Sarah

Ecclesiastes' "a time to weep, and. . ."

8
800 Pts

Pison
Hiddekel
Euphrates

9
900 Pts

priests of Nob
the sound of sheep and cattle
falling on own sword

10
1000 Pts

a shadow
swifter than a weaver's shuttle
a handbreadth

Answers on pages 239–240.

Your Score for This Quiz: ____
Running Total: ____

Quiz 30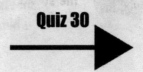

the serpent of Revelation
the wise and foolish builders
Noah

Judas Iscariot
Matthew
Phillip

**broken chains
shouts and cuts
a herd of pigs**

**King Saul, to David
the mighty Nimrod
the outdoorsy Esau**

**the seven spirits of God
before His throne
"Thy word"
five wise and five foolish virgins**

**Wonderful
Counsellor
The Prince of Peace**

**like a dog returning to its vomit
a rich man building bigger barns
the apostle Paul in his "glorying"**

**a story of a poor man's stolen lamb
King David's fury
"Thou art the man"**

9
900 Pts

**seedtime
white fields
few laborers**

10
1000 Pts

**Zin
Paran
Sinai**

Answers on page 240.

**Your Score for This Quiz: ____
Running Total: ____**

Quiz 31

1
100 Pts

a sister named Mary
the town of Bethany
a visit from Jesus

2
200 Pts

death of children
loss of property
painful boils

3
300 Pts

a parabolic Pharisee, twice a week

Queen Esther's Jews,
for three days

Jesus, for forty days

4
400 Pts

faith
meekness
temperance

5
500 Pts

"What is truth?"

"What I have written
I have written"

"I find no fault in him"

6
600 Pts

**Didymus
doubting the resurrection
"My Lord and my God"**

7
700 Pts

**scarlet sins washed clean
the glorified Jesus' hair
Gideon's fleece**

8
800 Pts

**Samson's foxes
Peter's denial of Jesus
Nadab and Abihu**

9
900 Pts

Judas Iscariot
Jesus' crucifixion companions
the second coming

10
1000 Pts

Abimelech's injury
Jezebel's remains
Golgotha

Answers on page 241.

Your Score for This Quiz: ____
Running Total: ____

Quiz 32

1
100 Pts

daytime darkness
mocking soldiers
two thieves

2
200 Pts

the dust of the ground
work in a garden
names for the animals

3
300 Pts

**a withered hand made well
a fig tree cursed
a coin found in a fish's mouth**

4
400 Pts

"Thou shalt never wash my feet"

"I know not this man"

**"Thou hast the words
of eternal life"**

5
500 Pts

**Queen Vashti deposed
a mocker
Jesus' first miracle**

**Alexander and Rufus
a Cyrenian
carrying Jesus' cross**

**Uzzah's death
the Ten Commandments
gold plating**

**King Ahab
Baal worship
Naboth's vineyard**

9
900 Pts

a broken spirit's effects
a vision of Ezekiel
the creation of Eve

10
1000 Pts

Moses' serpent, lifted up
Saul's helmet, refused by David
Jesus' feet, in Revelation

Answers on pages 241–242.

Your Score for This Quiz: ____
Running Total: ____

Quiz 33

1
100 Pts

James
Simon the Canaanite
Thomas

2
200 Pts

the village of Bethany
sickness and death
resurrection

3
300 Pts

your adversary
the tempter
the enemy

4
400 Pts

the Transfiguration
Gethsemane
the isle of Patmos

5
500 Pts

Abba
"which art in heaven"
the commandment to honor

6
600 Pts

**Elijah
Haggai
Daniel**

7
700 Pts

**King Og
King Saul
Goliath**

8
800 Pts

**Chisleu
Sebat
Sivan**

9
900 Pts

the clouds, to God
Jehu, who "driveth furiously"
an Ethiopian eunuch, reading Isaiah

10
1000 Pts

mint
anise
cummin

Answers on page 242.

Your Score for This Quiz: ___
Running Total: ___

Quiz 34

1
100 Pts

love
joy
peace

2
200 Pts

a tiller of the ground
a murderer
a marked man

700 wives
1,005 songs
3,000 proverbs

Lamech and Noah
Jesse and David
Abraham and Issac

Adam and Eve at creation
Job at birth
a disciple at the crucifixion

6
600 Pts

**Abana
Pharpar
Euphrates**

7
700 Pts

**the sign on Jesus' cross
the tower of Babel
the disciples at Pentecost**

8
800 Pts

**Samson's wife
King Abimelech
Goliath**

9
900 Pts

**a Jewish ruler
a nighttime visit with Jesus
"Ye must be born again"**

10
1000 Pts

**an Elkoshite
a vision
the destruction of Nineveh**

Answers on pages 242–243.

Your Score for This Quiz: ___
Running Total: ___

Quiz 35

1
100 Pts

the pure in heart
the merciful
they that mourn

2
200 Pts

a shepherd boy
jealous brothers
a coat of many colors

skins for clothing
the sweat of the brow
cherubim with a flaming sword

the Jordan River
"Thou art my beloved Son"
John the Baptist

Pharez and Zarah

Jacob and Esau

the beloved's breasts in
Song of Solomon

3
300 Pts

4
400 Pts

5
500 Pts

6
600 Pts

a rainbow
four beasts
twenty-four elders

7
700 Pts

sired Methuselah
walked with God
disappeared without dying

8
800 Pts

Nabal the Carmelite
correcting an insult
marriage to a future king

9
900 Pts

king of Israel
Baal worship
Jezebel

10
1000 Pts

Evil-Merodach
Cyrus
Nebuchadnezzar

Answers on pages 243–244.

Your Score for This Quiz: ____
Running Total: ____

Quiz 36

1
100 Pts

using spit to heal a blind man
raising Lazarus to life
walking on water

2
200 Pts

spies in Canaan

leftovers at the feeding of
the five thousand

young Jesus at the temple court

3
300 Pts

**Son of Man
Son of David
Son of God**

 4
400 Pts

**a murder plot
Midianite merchants
the Egyptian official Potiphar**

 5
500 Pts

Israelite brick makers in Egypt

the apostle Paul, three times

**Jesus, at the hands of
Roman soldiers**

6
600 Pts

a paralyzed man lowered
through a roof

the plague of frogs on Egypt

undefiled in marriage

7
700 Pts

people who refuse the
mark of the beast

John the Baptist

the fallen Goliath

8
800 Pts

"How shall we escape, if we neglect
so great salvation?"

"There remaineth therefore a rest
to the people of God"

"Not forsaking the assembling of
ourselves together"

9
900 Pts

bath
cor
homer

10
1000 Pts

Amplias
Nymphas
Andronicus

Answers on page 244.

Your Score for This Quiz: ____
Running Total: ____

Quiz 37

1
100 Pts

twelve tribes
also known as Jacob
God's chosen people

2
200 Pts

"Who is my neighbor?"
a band of thieves
bandages, oil, and wine

3
300 Pts

"Thou that killest the prophets"
"Pray for the peace of. . ."
"The holy city"

4
400 Pts

Nun and Joshua
Amittai and Jonah
God and Jesus

5
500 Pts

Cleopas, on the road to Emmaus
"Doubting" Thomas
more than 500 believers

6
600 Pts

"All have sinned, and come short
of the glory of God"

"I am not ashamed of the gospel"

"The gift of God is eternal life"

7
700 Pts

Caiaphas, in Jesus' time
Hilkiah, in King Josiah's time
Jesus, for all Christians

8
800 Pts

"Render to Caesar the things
that are Caesar's"

money in a fish's mouth

Joseph and Mary's journey to
Bethlehem

9
900 Pts

Omri
Ahaziah
Jehoahaz

10
1000 Pts

the Israelites,
in their slavery in Egypt

the creation, because of sin

the Spirit's intercession
for Christians

Answers on page 245.

Your Score for This Quiz: ____
Running Total: ____

Quiz 38

1
100 Pts

King Herod
a star in the east
gifts for the baby Jesus

2
200 Pts

Holy One of Israel
the Father of lights
I AM

3
300 Pts

the governor of Judaea
clemency for Barabbas
the crucifixion of Jesus

4
400 Pts

light
Heaven
Earth

5
500 Pts

a bright light
the voice of Jesus
the road to Damascus

6
600 Pts

a nobleman's son healed
Nathanael's hometown
water turned into wine

7
700 Pts

the lovers' bed in Song of Solomon
plants for food, before the fall
the pastures of Psalm 23

8
800 Pts

the seventh plague on Egypt

the seventh vial judgment
of Revelation

the Roman soldiers' mocking
greeting to Jesus

9
900 Pts

mint, anise, and cummin
Abraham and Melchizedek
the windows of heaven

10
1000 Pts

stoned
slain with the sword
sawn asunder

Answers on pages 245–246.

Your Score for This Quiz: ___
Running Total: ___

Quiz 39

1
100 Pts

believer in Jesus
brother of Jesus
betrayer of Jesus

2
200 Pts

Chief Shepherd
Lamb of God
Lion of the tribe of Juda

the hairy Esau
sin, according to Isaiah
a parted sea

complaining, hungry Israelites
dew
bread from heaven

sons Joseph and Benjamin
husband Jacob
sister Leah

6
600 Pts

the prodigal son's father

Peter and John,
to Jesus' empty tomb

Philip, to the Ethiopian eunuch

7
700 Pts

the plain of Jordan
Sodom
Zoar

8
800 Pts

Othniel
Jair
Elon

Nissi
Shalom
Jireh

Habakkuk's vision
John's revelation
Israel's defeat of the Amalekites

Answers on page 246.

Your Score for This Quiz: ___
Running Total: ___

Quiz 40

1
100 Pts

**Ephratah
a filled inn
the birthplace of Jesus**

2
200 Pts

**the captain of the host of the Lord
Joshua
walking around a city for seven days**

3
300 Pts

"Hosanna"
"Hail, King of the Jews!"
"Crucify him"

4
400 Pts

a man journeying to a far country

five, two, and one

"Well done, thou good
and faithful servant"

5
500 Pts

father Bethuel
husband Isaac
sons Jacob and Esau

the beloved's black hair in Song of Solomon

Elijah's miraculous source of food

Noah's flood reconnaissance

a king's great feast

gold and silver vessels from the Jerusalem temple

"MENE, MENE, TEKEL, UPHARSIN"

unclean
seducing
ministering

9
900 Pts

Teresh
Zeresh
Hatach

10
1000 Pts

Cyrus
Darius
Artaxerxes

Answers on page 247.

Your Score for This Quiz: ____
Running Total: ____

Quiz 41

1
100 Pts

**King of the Jews
the house and lineage of David
swaddling clothes**

2
200 Pts

**the pharisee and the tax collector
the rich man and Lazarus
the lost sheep**

**the Jordan River
"O generation of vipers"
unworthy to untie Christ's sandals**

**a hungry hunter
red pottage (stew)
the price of a birthright**

**a fruit of the Spirit
Jesus gives not as the world gives
something to pray for Jerusalem**

6
600 Pts

**Joseph in Egypt
Samson in Gaza
Paul and Silas in Philippi**

7
700 Pts

**"Go to the ant, thou sluggard"
"A soft answer turneth away wrath"
"Trust in the LORD with
all thine heart"**

8
800 Pts

**earrings
an idol
ground to powder**

9
900 Pts

King Uzziah
Maher-Shalal-Hash-Baz
the son of Amoz

10
1000 Pts

red
black
pale

Answers on pages 247–248.

Your Score for This Quiz: ____
Running Total: ____

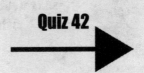

Quiz 42

1
100 Pts

harpist
psalm writer
giant killer

2
200 Pts

remember the Sabbath day
don't steal
don't commit adultery

3
300 Pts

husband Jacob
sons Reuben and Simeon
sister Rachel

4
400 Pts

"Wine is a mocker"

"Open rebuke is better
than secret love"

"A wise son maketh a glad father"

5
500 Pts

food
drink
clothing

6
600 Pts

holes for sleeping
Samson's fire
Jesus' appraisal of King Herod

7
700 Pts

"the power of God unto salvation"

a command to preach to
every creature

Paul's mystery to be made known

8
800 Pts

Hagar, to Sarah
Bilhah, to Rachel
the virgin Mary, to the Lord

the queen of Sheba's questions for Solomon

understanding Paul's writings, according to Peter

Pharaoh's heart

**a proud look
a lying tongue
hands that shed innocent blood**

Answers on page 248.

Your Score for This Quiz: ___
Running Total: ___

Quiz 43

1
100 Pts

the first and the last
the light of the world
the way, the truth, and the life

2
200 Pts

long hair
great strength
Delilah

3
300 Pts

"Man shall not live by bread alone, but by every word of God"

"Thou shalt worship the Lord thy God, and him only shalt thou serve"

"Thou shalt not tempt the Lord thy God"

4
400 Pts

Arioch
King Darius
Meschach

5
500 Pts

wine mingled with myrrh
the crucifixion
"the place of a skull"

"the breastplate of righteousness"
"feet shod with the preparation
of the gospel of peace"
"the sword of the Spirit"

King David's palace
the behemoth's tail
Lebanon

wise men visit the baby Jesus

Mary, Joseph, and Jesus
flee to Egypt

an earthquake accompanies
the opening of Jesus' empty tomb

9
900 Pts

divisions
lawsuits
a man has his father's wife

10
1000 Pts

a letter from the apostle Paul
a riot over the goddess Diana
a first love forsaken

Answers on page 249.

Your Score for This Quiz: ____
Running Total: ____

Quiz 44

1
100 Pts

**walking on water
"Feed my sheep"
a letter to God's "elect"**

2
200 Pts

**water turned into wine
a storm calmed
ten lepers cleansed**

3
300 Pts

**Peter, James, and John
Moses and Elijah
a shining Jesus**

4
400 Pts

**Manoah
a Nazarite vow
the pillars of Dagon's house**

5
500 Pts

**Jethro
Pharaoh
Joshua**

6
600 Pts

the brook of Eshcol
a large cluster of grapes
Joshua and Caleb

7
700 Pts

Jesus turns water into wine

Jesus tells Nicodemus,
"Ye must be born again"

the death and resurrection of Lazarus

8
800 Pts

seals
trumpets
vials, or bowls

9
900 Pts

a centurion named Julius
Euroclydon
a shipwreck

10
1000 Pts

a Temanite
a Naamathite
a Shuhite

Answers on pages 249–250.

Your Score for This Quiz: ____
Running Total: ____

1
100 Pts

the substance of things hoped for
without works, is dead
the just shall live by

2
200 Pts

midday darkness
a centurion praising God
"Into thy hands I commend my spirit"

**Jesus in Samaria
a request for a drink
five husbands**

**Matthat
Heli
Joseph the carpenter**

**a fruit of the Spirit
a characteristic of Moses
to inherit the earth**

6
600 Pts

Jesus' ascension into heaven
the Holy Spirit's arrival at Pentecost
the deaths of Ananias and Sapphira

7
700 Pts

wars and rumors of wars

famines, pestilences,
and earthquakes

false prophets

8
800 Pts

Joanna the wife of Chuza
Susanna
Mary Magdalene

9
900 Pts

Maachah
Haggith
Eglah

10
1000 Pts

"feet that be swift in running to mischief"

"a false witness that speaketh lies"

"he that soweth discord among brethren"

Answers on page 250.

Your Score for This Quiz: ____
Running Total: ____

Quiz 46

1
100 Pts

created in God's image
dominion over fish, fowl, and cattle
"Be fruitful, and multiply"

2
200 Pts

Jesus' invitation to "come and dine"
Peter's catch of 153
Jonah's "great" specimen

3
300 Pts

Carmel
Hermon
Zion

4
400 Pts

Noah found it
God's is sufficient
come boldly to the throne of

5
500 Pts

a donkey and a colt

clothes and branches
on the roadway

people shouting, "Hosanna!"

a great mystery
profitable unto all things
with contentment, is great gain

when fathers eat sour grapes
eye for eye. . .
gnashing

two witnesses are killed
and resurrected in Jerusalem

Satan is bound for
one thousand years

God wipes tears from believers' eyes

9
900 Pts

Jabbok
Ulai
Kishon

10
1000 Pts

liars and evil beasts
the harbor of Phenice (Phoenix)
Titus's parish

Answers on page 251.

Your Score for This Quiz: ___
Running Total: ___

Quiz 47

1
100 Pts

roasted meat
unleavend bread
eating in haste

2
200 Pts

a nephew in danger
a wife who laughed
a God with a promise

3
300 Pts

water turned to blood
dust turned to lice
ashes turned to boils

4
400 Pts

"The Son of man hath not where to lay his head"

"Let the dead bury their dead"

"No man, having put his hand to the plough, and looking back, is fit for the kingdom of God"

5
500 Pts

Paul, at Cenchrea

Absalom, when it became too heavy

Samson, by way of Delilah

6
600 Pts

a little for Timothy's stomach
none for the Nazarite
". . .but be filled with the Spirit"

7
700 Pts

John the Baptist is born

angels tell shepherds of
the birth of Jesus

Mary and Joseph lose twelve-year-old
Jesus at the temple

8
800 Pts

son of Jephunneh
associate of Joshua
a positive report from Canaan

9
900 Pts

**Hor
Tabor
Moriah**

10
1000 Pts

**Tabitha
helping the poor
death and resurrection**

Answers on pages 251–252.

**Your Score for This Quiz: ___
Running Total: ___**

196

Quiz 48

1
100 Pts

birth in Egypt
flight to Midian
death on Mt. Nebo

2
200 Pts

husband Zechariah
son John
cousin Mary

3
300 Pts

Haman, to the Jews
a command to love
Christ's footstool

4
400 Pts

the Israelites' "pillar"
the lake of the second death
Elijah's challenge to
the prophets of Baal

5
500 Pts

Jesus' invitation to Thomas
handwriting on the wall
a giant of Gath's "extras"

Reuben, to Jacob
Esau, to Isaac
lost in the last plague on Egypt

the Word of God, figuratively
Peter and Malchus
future plowshares

"My soul doth magnify the Lord"

"He that is mighty
hath done to me great things"

"All generations shall call me blessed"

9
900 Pts

**the death of Judas Iscariot
eleven apostles
the drawing of lots**

10
1000 Pts

**"Behold, what manner of love the
Father hath bestowed upon us"**

"God is love"

**"We love him, because
he first loved us"**

Answers on page 252.

**Your Score for This Quiz: ____
Running Total: ____**

Quiz 49

1
100 Pts

a servant girl
an oath, cursing, and swearing
a cock's crowing

2
200 Pts

Moriah
tools for a burnt offering
a ram caught in a thicket

3
300 Pts

**beautiful on the mountains
a sinful woman's kiss for Jesus
God's Word as a lamp**

4
400 Pts

**Jesse's sons
Josiah's coronation
people on the ark**

5
500 Pts

the earth quakes and rocks split

**graves open and the bodies
of saints come back to life**

**the veil of the temple
tears from top to bottom**

6
600 Pts

**nurture
admonition
provoke not to wrath**

7
700 Pts

**Magog
Babylon
Armageddon**

8
800 Pts

**Jerub-Baal
Boanerges
Barnabas**

9
900 Pts

fornicators
idolators
thieves

10
1000 Pts

Sisera
a drink of milk
a lethal tent nail

Answers on page 253.

Your Score for This Quiz: ____
Running Total: ____

Quiz 50

1
100 Pts

**immortal
invisible
the only wise**

2
200 Pts

**go into all the world
teach all nations
baptize**

3
300 Pts

graven
man made in God's
Christ, of the invisible God

4
400 Pts

spitting
striking
a crown of thorns

5
500 Pts

Jephthah's daughter

Mary, at the time of
the angel's visit

ten women in a parable of Jesus

Saul's persecution
Christ is the head
built on a rock

Abel's cries out from the ground
a woman with a twelve-year "issue"
Moses' sprinkling on the altar

a quarrel with John the Baptist
a daughter who danced
a head in a charger

9
900 Pts

Lot's wife
Paul's bonds
the Sabbath day, to keep it holy

10
1000 Pts

herbs to accompany
the Passover lamb

Peter's weeping after denying Jesus

the Israelites' water at Marah

Answers on pages 253–254.

Your Score for This Quiz: ____
Running Total: ____

Quiz 51

1
100 Pts

mite
farthing
penny

2
200 Pts

brother of Jesus
son of Alphaeus
son of Zebedee

3
300 Pts

a napkin
linen clothes
an empty tomb

 4
400 Pts

a city of Galilee
Nathanael's insulting question
Jesus' boyhood home

 5
500 Pts

corruptible versus incorruptible
Jesus' thorns
cast before God's throne

6
600 Pts

shittim, or acacia, wood
a pure gold overlay
two cherubim

7
700 Pts

Achor
Hinnom
the shadow of death

8
800 Pts

the sixth plague on Egypt

Hezekiah's illness,
healed with a lump of figs

Job and his potsherd

9
900 Pts

names covering the
scarlet beast of Revelation

Caiaphas's charge against Jesus

against the Holy Spirit, unforgivable

10
1000 Pts

"the man that walketh not in the
counsel of the ungodly"

"he whose transgression is forgiven"

"the nation whose God is the LORD"

Answers on page 254.

**Your Score for This Quiz: ____
Running Total: ____**

Quiz 52

1
100 Pts

span
cubit
furlong

2
200 Pts

from above
the true vine
the Alpha and Omega

3
300 Pts

don't covet house,
wife, or anything else

love as yourself

"Go, and do thou likewise"

4
400 Pts

a priest in Nehemiah's day
a warrior in David's army
the weeping prophet

5
500 Pts

the apostle Paul's haircut
Jephthah and his daughter
the childless Hannah

6
600 Pts

a son of David by Abigail

an Israelite who renewed the
covenant with Nehemiah

a prophet in a lion's den

7
700 Pts

Stephen is stoned to death
Saul is converted to faith in Jesus
an angel releases Peter from prison

8
800 Pts

"those servants, whom the lord when
he cometh shall find watching"

"the man that feareth the LORD"

"the man that endureth temptation"

9
900 Pts

On
Ur
Uz

10
1000 Pts

a beam in one's eye
a disfigured face during a fast
scribes and Pharisees

Answers on pages 254–255.

Your Score for This Quiz: ____
Running Total: ____

A perfect score for
*Bible Trivia Challenge:
Connect the Thots*
is 286,000 points. . . .
How well did you connect?

ANSWER
KEY

Quiz 1

1. olives (Matthew 24:3; Joshua 24:13; Genesis 8:11)

2. seventy (Daniel 9:24; Luke 10:1; Matthew 18:21–22)

3. people raised from the dead (2 Kings 4:32–37; Acts 20:9–12; John 11:43–44)

4. strong winds (Acts 2:1–2; Matthew 14:26–32; Job 1:18–19)

5. slaves (Genesis 39:1–3; Exodus 2:23; Philemon 10–16)

6. seven (Revelation 1:20; Acts 6:1–6; Genesis 7:2)

7. relatives of Moses (Exodus 4:14; Exodus 2:21–22; Numbers 26:59)

8. army commanders (2 Kings 5:1; 1 Chronicles 11:6; Judges 4:4–9)

9. characters in the book of Nehemiah (Nehemiah 4:3; Nehemiah 8:2; Nehemiah 2:1)

10. the tongue (James 3:6; James 3:8; James 3:6)

Quiz 2

1. objects in Jesus' parables (Matthew 13:47–50; Matthew 13:45–46; Matthew 13:31–32)

2. twelve (Matthew 10:1; Genesis 49:28; Revelation 21:21)

3. men named Simon (Matthew 10:2; Acts 9:43; Acts 8:9)

4. names of Satan (John 8:44; Revelation 12:9–10; Matthew 12:24)

5. judges of Israel (Judges 16:30–31; Judges 4:4; Judges 3:15)

6. characters in the book of Esther (Esther 2:5; Esther 1:9; Esther 3:1)

7. sites of earthquakes (Acts 16:12–26; Matthew 28:2; Exodus 19:18)

8. authors of proverbs (Proverbs 1:1; Proverbs 30:1; Proverbs 31:1)

9. cousins (1 Samuel 14:49–50; Esther 2:7; Luke 1:34–36)

10. metalworkers (Acts 19:24; 2 Chronicles 2:13–14; Genesis 4:22)

Quiz 3

1. women named Mary (John 19:25; John 11:2; Matthew 1:18)

2. the sin of Adam and Eve (Genesis 3:7; Genesis 3:17; Genesis 3:19)

3. golden things (Esther 8:1–4; Exodus 32:2–4; Revelation 21:2, 21)

4. seven (Genesis 29:20; Matthew 15:35–38; 2 Kings 5:10–11)

5. false gods (Acts 19:27; Judges 8:33; 1 Samuel 5:2–5)

6. husbands and wives (Ruth 1:3–5, 4:10; Acts 5:1; Genesis 24:67)

7. people who died by hanging (Esther 7:10; Matthew 27:3–5; Genesis 40:20–22)

8. places with towers (Genesis 11:5–9; Luke 13:4; 2 Chronicles 26:9)

9. seals (Ephesians 1:13; Revelation 6:1–8; Daniel 12:4)

10. things that withered (Isaiah 40:7; Matthew 21:18–19; Matthew 12:9–13)

Quiz 4

1. the temptation of Christ (Matthew 4:1–11)

2. mountains (Deuteronomy 34:1; Genesis 8:4; Exodus 19:20)

3. brothers (1 Samuel 17:28; Genesis 25:24–26; Matthew 4:21)

4. events in Joshua's life (Deuteronomy 13:16; Joshua 10:13–15; Joshua 6:26–27)

5. queens (Esther 2:17; 1 Kings 16:29–31; 2 Chronicles 22:10–12)

6. the armor of God (Ephesians 6:13–17)

7. Nebuchadnezzar's dream of a statue (Daniel 2:31–33)

8. nighttime visitors (John 3:1–2; Luke 2:8–9; Genesis 19:1)

9. sources of water (Exodus 17:6; Revelation 22:1; Genesis 26:19)

10. kings (1 Samuel 11:15; Numbers 21:33; Acts 25:13)

Quiz 5

1. measurements of weight (Genesis 24:22; 2 Samuel 12:30; John 19:39)

2. Esau (Genesis 25:25; Genesis 25:27; Genesis 27:36)

3. men named Zechariah (Luke 1:59–60; Zechariah 1:1; Matthew 23:35)

4. snakes (Genesis 3:1; Acts 28:1–3; Exodus 7:10–11)

5. shepherds (1 Samuel 16:11–13; Amos 1:1; John 10:14)

6. harlots, or prostitutes (Hebrews 11:31; Hosea 1:2–3, 3:1–3, Revelation 17:1–3)

7. thorns (Genesis 3:18; 2 Corinthians 12:7; Matthew 27:27–29)

8. lepers (2 Chronicles 26:21; Numbers 12:10; 2 Kings 5:1)

9. coworkers with Paul (Acts 15:40; Galatians 2:1; 2 Timothy 4:11)

10. oldest people of the Bible (Genesis 5:5; Genesis 5:20; Genesis 5:27)

Quiz 6

1. men named John (Matthew 3:1; Matthew 10:2; Acts 12:12)

2. calves (Exodus 32:4; Luke 15:23–24; Isaiah 11:6)

3. Samson (Judges 15:15–16; Judges 14:12; Judges 16:1)

4. places Jesus lived (Matthew 2:13–15; Matthew 4:12–13; Luke 4:14–16)

5. things that burn (Revelation 19:20; Genesis 8:20; Exodus 3:2)

6. spears (1 Samuel 19:10; John 19:33–34; Isaiah 2:4)

7. brothers of Jesus (Matthew 13:53–55)

8. rivers (2 Kings 5:12; Genesis 2:10–11; Matthew 3:6)

9. Samuel (1 Samuel 3:2–5; 1 Samuel 3:20; 1 Samuel 28:8–15)

10. singing (Acts 16:25; Mark 14:26; Exodus 15:1)

Quiz 7

1. the story of Noah and the ark (Genesis 8:8–9; Genesis 9:16–17; Genesis 8:1–4)

2. Luke (2 Timothy 4:11; Luke 1:3; Colossians 4:14)

3. weddings (John 2:1; Revelation 19:7; Matthew 22:1–2)

4. camels (Genesis 24:64; Matthew 23:24; Luke 18:25)

5. brothers (1 Chronicles 20:5; Genesis 22:21; Matthew 4:18)

6. Lydia (Acts 16:12–15)

7. people healed by Jesus (Mark 10:46–52; Luke 4:38–39; Mark 5:21–43)

8. people who rode donkeys (Matthew 21:6–7; Judges 10:3–4; Numbers 22:22–23)

9. authors of Psalms (Psalm 3; Psalm 90; Psalm 73)

10. censuses (1 Chronicles 21:1; Numbers 26:1–2; Luke 2:1)

Quiz 8

1. gifts for the baby Jesus (Matthew 2:1–11)

2. the story of Jonah (Jonah 4:7–8; Jonah 1:17; Jonah 4:11)

3. publicans, or tax collectors (Matthew 10:3; Luke 19:2; Luke 18:13)

4. Bathsheba (2 Samuel 11:2; 2 Samuel 11:3; 2 Samuel 12:24–25)

5. martyrs (Matthew 14:3–10; Acts 12:1–2; Acts 7:59–60)

6. elements of dreams interpreted by Joseph (Genesis 40:8–19)

7. witchcraft, or sorcery (2 Kings 9:22; Acts 13:8; 1 Samuel 28:7)

8. pearls (Revelation 21:21; Matthew 13:45; Matthew 7:6)

9. things that fell (1 Samuel 5:1–5; Luke 10:18; Joshua 6:1–20)

10. people accused of drunkenness (Luke 7:34; 1 Samuel 1:12–14; Acts 2:1–13)

Quiz 9

1. Psalm 23 (Psalm 23:1; Psalm 23:2; Psalm 23:5)

2. John the Baptist (Matthew 3:4)

3. Jesus' Sermon on the Mount (Matthew 5:1–7)

4. murderers (Genesis 4:8; Mark 15:7; John 8:44)

5. salt (Genesis 14:3; Colossians 4:6; Genesis 19:23–26)

6. family line of David (1 Chronicles 2:12–15)

7. kinds of hearts (Proverbs 17:22; Jeremiah 17:9; Exodus 7:14)

8. Samaritans (John 4:6–9; Luke 17:11–16; Luke 10:25–37)

9. people with fevers (Job 30:30; Acts 28:8; Matthew 8:14)

10. second sons (1 Chronicles 2:13; Genesis 4:1–2; Genesis 25:24–26)

Quiz 10

1. Simon Peter (Mark 14:37–38; Luke 5:4–9; Mark 14:72)

2. Joseph (Genesis 37:3; Genesis 37:5–7; Genesis 37:3)

3. sayings of Jesus on the cross (John 19:28; Luke 23:34; Mark 15:34)

4. the prophet Elijah (1 Kings 17:7–13; 1 Kings 17:1–6; 1 Kings 18:16–22)

5. fathers and sons (Matthew 4:21; 2 Samuel 3:2–4; Genesis 16:15)

6. King Saul (1 Samuel 9:3; 1 Samuel 10:21–23; 1 Samuel 10:1)

7. beautiful women (Esther 1:11; Esther 2:7; Genesis 29:17)

8. people who were stoned (Acts 14:19; Joshua 7:24–26; Acts 7:59)

9. people who danced (2 Samuel 6:14; Exodus 15:20; Matthew 14:6)

10. children of prophets (Hosea 1:6; Hosea 1:9; Isaiah 8:3)

Quiz 11

1. "I am" statements of Jesus (John 6:35; John 15:1; Revelation 1:8)

2. the Ten Commandments (Exodus 20:1–17)

3. cities in the story of Jonah (Jonah 1:1–3)

4. men named Simon (Matthew 13:55; Matthew 27:32; Matthew 10:4)

5. nonhuman things that spoke (Genesis 3:1; Exodus 3:1–4; Numbers 22:30)

6. people on roofs (Mark 2:1–4; 2 Samuel 11:2–3; Acts 10:9–16)

7. the casting of lots (Acts 1:26; Matthew 27:35; Jonah 1:7)

8. honey (Matthew 3:4; Judges 14:14–18; Exodus 3:17)

9. characters in the book of Job (Job 4:1; Job 20:1; Job 32:2)

10. whirlwinds (2 Kings 2:1; Job 38:1; Hosea 8:7)

Quiz 12

1. sisters (1 Chronicles 2:16; Luke 10:38–39; Genesis 29:16)

2. Caesars (Luke 3:1; Acts 11:28; Luke 2:1)

3. tongues (Acts 2:1–3; 1 Corinthians 14:13; James 3:8)

4. Abel (Genesis 4:1–8)

5. Paul (Acts 22:2–3; Acts 16:14; Acts 9:1–4)

6. stars (Matthew 2:1–2; Revelation 8:10–11; Genesis 1:16–19)

7. washing (2 Kings 5:11–14; Matthew 27:24; John 13:3–5)

8. giants (Numbers 13:33; 2 Samuel 21:16; 1 Samuel 17:4)

9. unclean animals (Leviticus 11:1–19)

10. ears (Deuteronomy 15:17; 2 Timothy 4:3; John 18:10)

Quiz 13

1. Judas Iscariot (Acts 1:18–19; Luke 22:47–48; Matthew 27:3–4)

2. Jacob (Genesis 29:20–25; Genesis 27:36; Genesis 28:10–12)

3. things in the book of Daniel (Daniel 8:1–8; Daniel 5:1–6; Daniel 3:1–15)

4. swine (Luke 15:11–16; Mark 5:9–13; Matthew 7:6)

5. men named Simeon (Genesis 29:28–33; Luke 2:25–32; Acts 13:1)

6. characters in the story of Ruth (Ruth 1:1–5)

7. widows (Luke 2:36–37; Mark 12:41–44; Luke 18:1–8)

8. governors (Genesis 42:1–6; Luke 2:2; Luke 3:1)

9. the book of Ecclesiastes (Ecclesiastes 11:1; Ecclesiastes 3:1; Ecclesiastes 1:2)

10. things relating to fools (Psalm 14:1; Proverbs 15:5; Proverbs 28:26)

Quiz 14

1. the Lord's Prayer (Matthew 6:9–13)

2. disciples of Jesus (Matthew 10:2–4)

3. blind people (Acts 9:3–8; Genesis 19:1–11; Mark 10:46)

4. asses, or donkeys (Matthew 21:6–11; 1 Samuel 9:3–4; Numbers 22:21–31)

5. rules for the Nazarite vow (Numbers 6:1–8)

6. feasts of Israel (Deuteronomy 16:16)

7. people whom God struck dead (Numbers 3:4; 2 Samuel 6:6–7; Acts 5:1–10)

8. prophetesses (Exodus 15:20; Luke 2:36; 2 Kings 22:14)

9. vineyards (1 Kings 21:15–16; Matthew 20:1–16; Genesis 9:20–21)

10. Barnabas (Acts 4:36; Acts 15:39–40; Acts 14:8–12)

Quiz 15

1. Babel (Genesis 10:32–11:9)

2. people who wept (Exodus 2:5–10; John 11:32–43; Luke 22:61–62)

3. people from whom demons were cast (Luke 8:2; Acts 16:16–18; Mark 5:1–13)

4. thirty (Judges 10:3–4; Luke 3:23; Matthew 27:3)

5. prophets (Acts 21:10; Habakkuk 1:1; 2 Samuel 7:2)

6. centurions (Luke 23:46–47; Acts 10:1; Matthew 8:5–13)

7. people famed for their hair (2 Samuel 14:25–26; Judges 16:13–17; John 11:1–2)

8. miracles of Elisha (2 Kings 6:1–7; 2 Kings 2:22–24; 2 Kings 4:32–37)

9. births foretold (Luke 1:30–31; Luke 1:13; Judges 13:2–24)

10. people who died by suicide (1 Kings 16:18; 1 Samuel 31:4; Matthew 27:3–5)

Quiz 16

1. David (1 Samuel 16:11–13; 1 Samuel 16:23; 2 Samuel 2:4)

2. John the Baptist (Luke 1:57–60; Matthew 14:1–10; Matthew 3:1–3)

3. people who were baptized (Acts 8:27–38; Acts 16:13–15; Mark 1:9)

4. land (Deuteronomy 9:28; Leviticus 20:24; Exodus 8:22)

5. barren women (Genesis 11:30; Genesis 29:31; Judges 13:2)

6. baskets (Genesis 40:16–17; Matthew 14:13–21; 2 Corinthians 11:30–33)

7. people who ate honey (Judges 14:5–9; 1 Samuel 14:27; Matthew 3:4)

8. baldness (2 Kings 2:22–23; Micah 1:16; Leviticus 21:1–5)

9. occurrences in caves (1 Samuel 24:3–4; 1 Kings 18:4; John 11:38–44)

10. people who asked God to kill them (1 Kings 19:1–4; Jonah 4:1–3; Numbers 11:4–15)

Quiz 17

1. Moses (Exodus 2:21; Numbers 14:26–34; Exodus 31:18)

2. Jonathan (1 Samuel 14:1; 1 Samuel 14:14; 1 Samuel 20:42)

3. places where wine was served (John 2:1–10; Esther 1:1–8; Genesis 9:20–21)

4. blood (Luke 22:39–44; Leviticus 17:11; Revelation 7:14–15)

5. wives of King David (1 Samuel 30:5; 1 Samuel 19:11)

6. tongues (Luke 16:19–24; Exodus 4:10; Acts 2:4)

7. high priests (Acts 23:2; John 18:13; Hebrews 3:1)

8. pleasure (Ezekiel 33:11; Hebrews 11:25; Psalm 16:11)

9. chariots (Exodus 14:28; 2 Chronicles 1:14; 2 Kings 2:11)

10. purple (John 19:1–3; Esther 8:15; Acts 16:14)

Quiz 18

1. sons of Noah (Genesis 6:10)

2. Abraham (Genesis 12:1–5)

3. visions of Ezekiel (Ezekiel 37:1; Ezekiel 40:5; Ezekiel 1:15–16)

4. Joshua (Numbers 27:18–20)

5. widows (2 Samuel 11:3, 26; 1 Samuel 25:36–38; Luke 2:36–37)

6. sayings of Job (Job 19:20; Job 1:21)

7. King Belshazzar (Daniel 5:1–6)

8. foods of Egypt, eaten by Israelite slaves (Numbers 11:5)

9. tetrarchs (Luke 3:1)

10. months of the Hebrew calendar (Exodus 13:4; Esther 3:7; Nehemiah 6:15)

Quiz 19

1. events in the book of Genesis (Genesis 1:1; Genesis 3:17–19; Genesis 12:1–3)

2. Jacob (Genesis 25:29–34; Genesis 32:24–28; Genesis 45:25–26)

3. small offerings to God (Mark 12:41–44; Leviticus 5:7; John 6:5–9)

4. Pharaoh (Exodus 6:13; Exodus 7:3; Exodus 11:1)

5. types of offerings (Exodus 29:14; Leviticus 6:6; Numbers 7:57)

6. tombs (Mark 5:1–9; Matthew 27:57–60; Matthew 23:27)

7. Nineveh (Genesis 10:8–11; Jonah 4:11; Jonah 1:1–2)

8. thunder (Mark 3:17; Exodus 20:1–18; Exodus 9:23–25)

9. the prophet Elijah (1 Kings 17:1; 1 Kings 18:1; 1 Kings 19:12–13)

10. stops on Paul's journey to Rome (Acts 27:8; Acts 28:12; Acts 28:15)

Quiz 20

1. men named Joseph (Matthew 1:24–25, 13:53–55; Genesis 45:26; Matthew 27:57)

2. forty days (Genesis 7:11–12; Luke 4:1–2; Acts 1:1–3)

3. Pentecost (Acts 1:26–2:4)

4. obey (Ephesians 6:1; 1 Samuel 15:22; Acts 5:29)

5. Bible study (Ezra 7:10; 2 Timothy 2:15; Acts 17:10–11)

6. lions (Judges 14:7–9; 1 Samuel 17:34–36; Revelation 5:5)

7. creatures in the book of Job (Job 39:1; Job 41:1; Job 40:15)

8. men named Ananias (Acts 5:1–5; Acts 9:17–19; Acts 23:1–2)

9. minor characters in the story of Esther (Esther 1:16; Esther 2:8: Esther 2:21)

10. unusual tools for healing (Acts 19:12; Acts 5:15)

Quiz 21

1. people Jesus blessed in His beatitudes (Matthew 5:1–10)

2. Joshua (Numbers 13:16; Numbers 14:6; Joshua 1:1–7)

3. three (Genesis 6:10; Matthew 26:75; Matthew 12:38–40)

4. events in the book of Esther (Esther 1:2–4; Esther 7:10; Esther 9:28)

5. King Saul (1 Samuel 18:20; 1 Samuel 9:27–10:1; 1 Samuel 28:5–7)

6. tents (Acts 18:1–3; Exodus 26:1–36; Judges 4:17–21)

7. people who won't inherit the kingdom of God (1 Corinthians 6:9–10)

8. things that are cursed (Genesis 3:14; Job 3:1; Galatians 3:13)

9. things that sting (1 Corinthians 15:56; Proverbs 23:32; Revelation 9:7–10)

10. the prophet Ezekiel (Ezekiel 2:1; Ezekiel 3:1; Ezekiel 3:17)

Quiz 22

1. Goliath (1 Samuel 17:8–51)

2. the story of Gideon (Judges 6:11–37)

3. things described as holy (2 Corinthians 13:12; 2 Timothy 3:15; Acts 2:4)

4. the story of Ruth (Ruth 1:3–5; Ruth 2:17; Ruth 4:6)

5. places of prayer (Matthew 6:6; Mark 14:32; Jonah 2:1)

6. Samuel (1 Samuel 1:19–25)

7. circumcision (Genesis 17:9–11; Luke 2:21; Genesis 34:1–25)

8. stops on Paul's missionary journeys (Acts 13:2–5)

9. wisdom (1 Corinthians 1:25; Proverbs 8:11; 1 Kings 3:6–28)

10. footstools (Isaiah 66:1; Matthew 22:41–45; James 2:3)

Quiz 23

1. titles of Jesus Christ (Revelation 19:13–16; John 1:29; Mark 1:1)

2. plagues on Egypt (Exodus 8:3; Exodus 10:21–22; Exodus 11:5)

3. Passover (Exodus 12:1–11)

4. fruit (Amos 8:1; Galatians 5:22–23; Genesis 2:17, 3:3)

5. compliments from the Song of Solomon (Song of Solomon 4:1; Song of Solomon 7:2; Song of Solomon 7:4)

6. harpists (Genesis 4:21; 1 Samuel 16:23; Revelation 5:6–8)

7. oil (Matthew 25:1–4; 1 Samuel 16:1–13; 1 Kings 17:7–12)

8. Miriam (Numbers 12:10; Exodus 15:20; Numbers 26:59)

9. people visited by the angel Gabriel (Daniel 8:15–16; Luke 1:18–19; Luke 1:26–27)

10. millstones (Judges 9:52–53; Deuteronomy 24:6; Matthew 18:6)

Quiz 24

1. the apostle Paul (1 Corinthians 15:9; Acts 9:1–6; 2 Corinthians 12:7)

2. parables of Jesus (Matthew 7:24–27; Mark 2:19–22; Matthew 18:21–35)

3. Andrew (Matthew 4:18)

4. churches of Revelation (Revelation 2:1; Revelation 2:8; Revelation 2:18)

5. Eli the priest (1 Samuel 2:11–12; 1 Samuel 4:16–18)

6. three hundred (1 Kings 11:1–3; Judges 7:7; Genesis 5:22)

7. Philip the evangelist (Acts 21:8; Acts 8:26–30; Acts 21:9)

8. constellations mentioned in the book of Job (Job 9:9)

9. things the apostle Paul wanted in prison (2 Timothy 4:13)

10. Bible characters who appear as children (1 Samuel 1:21–28; Luke 2:41–52; 2 Chronicles 34:1)

Quiz 25

1. Moses (Matthew 17:1–3; Numbers 14:26–35; Exodus 20:1–21)

2. James and John (Matthew 4:21)

3. death (Romans 8:6; Job 30:23; Romans 6:23)

4. churches of Revelation (Revelation 2:12; Revelation 3:1; Revelation 3:7)

5. Paul's sufferings as an apostle (2 Corinthians 11:25–27)

6. destroyers of earthly treasure; according to Jesus (Matthew 6:19)

7. the story of Gideon (Judges 7:1–13)

8. coworkers with the apostle Paul (Colossians 4:10; Colossians 4:7; Romans 16:3)

9. things to abstain from (Acts 15:29; 1 Thessalonians 5:22; 1 Peter 2:11)

10. consequences of manipulating God's Word (Proverbs 30:6; Revelation 22:18; Revelation 22:19)

Quiz 26

1. arks (Exodus 2:1–4; Numbers 10:33; Genesis 6:13–14)

2. characters in the book of Daniel (Daniel 1:3–7)

3. parables of Jesus (Luke 13:6–9; Luke 15:8–10; Matthew 25:31–46)

4. the Sabbath (Exodus 20:8–11)

5. mountains (Exodus 33:6; 2 Samuel 1:6; Judges 9:7)

6. Boaz (Ruth 4:13–22)

7. the audible voice of God (John 12:12–29; Matthew 17:1–5; Matthew 3:13–17)

8. adultery (Exodus 20:14; Matthew 5:28; Matthew 19:9)

9. winepresses (Matthew 21:33; Judges 6:11; Revelation 14:19)

10. the prophet Ezekiel (Ezekiel 4:15; Ezekiel 5:1–2; Ezekiel 4:4–5)

Quiz 27

1. Adam and Eve (Genesis 3:11–24: 25)

2. the parable of the lost (prodigal) son (Luke 15:11–24)

3. Abraham or Abram (Genesis 25:1; Genesis 17:23; Genesis 15:18)

4. Mark (Colossians 4:10; 2 Timothy 4:11; Mark)

5. fiery things (Ephesians 6:16; 1 Peter 4:12; Daniel 3:19–20)

6. Solomon (2 Samuel 12:24–25; 2 Chronicles 9:20–21; 1 Kings 3:16–27)

7. dreams of Joseph (Genesis 37:2–11)

8. Ishmael (Genesis 16:15; Genesis 21:14; Genesis 16:11–12)

9. qualifications for deacons (1 Timothy 3:8–12)

10. victims of assassination (Judges 3:12–25; 2 Kings 12:19–20; 2 Kings 19:36–37)

Quiz 28

1. Noah (Genesis 7:13–16)

2. miracles of Jesus (Matthew 14:13–21; Mark 5:22–42; Luke 5:1–6)

3. Aaron (Exodus 4:14; Exodus 7:10; Exodus 32:2–4)

4. fruit of the spirit (Galatians 5:22–23)

5. lambs (Genesis 22:1–8; 2 Samuel 12:1–4; John 1:29)

6. rods (Hebrews 9:4; Proverbs 22:15; Revelation 19:15–16)

7. worms (Jonah 4:6–8; Acts 12:21–23; Mark 9:44–46)

8. "woe" pronounced by Jesus (Luke 11:44; Matthew 23:16; Luke 10:13)

9. descriptions of life (Genesis 47:9; Ecclesiastes 6:12; James 4:14)

10. the prophet Joel (Joel 1:4; Joel 3:14; Joel 2:28)

Quiz 29

1. the feeding of the five thousand (Matthew 14:13–21)

2. Sodom (Genesis 18:22–33; Genesis 19:24)

3. brothers (Exodus 7:1; Genesis 42:4; Genesis 4:8)

4. life (Revelation 2:7; Revelation 2:10; Revelation 3:5)

5. kisses (Genesis 29:10–11; 1 Samuel 20:41–42; Mark 14:44–45)

6. vial, or bowl, judgments of Revelation (Revelation 16:2–8)

7. laughter (Luke 8:52–53; Genesis 17:17, 18:12; Ecclesiastes 3:4)

8. rivers of Eden (Genesis 2:10–14)

9. King Saul (1 Samuel 22:6–19; 1 Samuel 15:1–14; 1 Samuel 31:1–4)

10. descriptions of the days of life (1 Chronicles 29:15; Job 7:6; Psalm 39:5)

Quiz 30

1. floods (Revelation 12:15–16; Luke 6:47–49; Genesis 7:6)

2. disciples of Jesus (Matthew 10:2–4)

3. the demoniac "Legion" (Mark 5:1–13)

4. hunters (1 Samuel 24:8–11; Genesis 10:9; Genesis 25:27)

5. lamps (Revelation 4:5; Psalm 119:105; Matthew 25:1–13)

6. Isaiah's prophecy of Christ (Isaiah 9:6)

7. fools (Proverbs 26:11; Luke 12:16–21; 2 Corinthians 12:11)

8. the prophet Nathan (2 Samuel 12:1–9)

9. harvest (Genesis 8:22; John 4:35; Matthew 9:37)

10. wildernesses, or deserts (Numbers 33:36; Genesis 21:21; Exodus 19:1)

Quiz 31

1. Martha (Luke 10:38–39; John 11:1; Luke 10:40–41)

2. sufferings of Job (Job 1:18–19; Job 1:16–17; Job 2:7)

3. people who fasted (Luke 18:9–12; Esther 4:15–16; Matthew 4:1–2)

4. fruit of the spirit (Galatians 5:22–23)

5. statements of Pontius Pilate (John 18:38; John 19:22; John 19:4)

6. the apostle Thomas (John 20:24–28)

7. wool (Isaiah 1:18; Revelation 1:12–18; Judges 6:36–38)

8. fire (Judges 15:3–5; Luke 22:54–57; Leviticus 10:1–2)

9. thieves (John 12:4–6; Mark 15:25–27; Revelation 3:3)

10. skulls (Judges 9:52–53; 2 Kings 9:34–37; Mark 15:22)

Quiz 32

1. the crucifixion of Jesus (Mark 15:16–33)

2. Adam (Genesis 2:7; Genesis 2:15; Genesis 2:19)

3. miracles of Jesus (Luke 6:6–10; Matthew 21:18–22; Matthew 17:24–27)

4. quotations of Simon Peter (John 13:8; Mark 14:71; John 6:68)

5. wine (Esther 1:10–19; Proverbs 20:1; John 2:1–11)

6. Simon (Mark 15:21)

7. the ark of the covenant (2 Samuel 6:6–7; Deuteronomy 10:1–5; Exodus 37:1–2)

8. Jezebel (1 Kings 16:29–31; 1 Kings 21:7)

9. bones (Proverbs 17:22; Ezekiel 37:1; Genesis 2:21–23)

10. brass, or bronze, things (Numbers 21:9; 1 Samuel 17:38–39; Revelation 2:18)

Quiz 33

1. disciples of Jesus (Matthew 10:2–4)

2. Lazarus (John 11:1–44)

3. names of the devil (1 Peter 5:8; Matthew 4:1–3; Matthew 13:39)

4. John (Matthew 17:1–2; Mark 14:32–33; Revelation 1:9)

5. father (Romans 8:15; Mathew 6:9; Exodus 20:12)

6. prophets (1 Kings 18:36; Haggai 2:1; Matthew 24:15)

7. tall men (Deuteronomy 3:11; 1 Samuel 9:2; 1 Samuel 17:4)

8. months of the Hebrew calendar (Nehemiah 1:1; Zechariah 1:7; Esther 8:9)

9. chariots (Psalm 104:3; 2 Kings 9:14–20; Acts 8:27–28)

10. spices tithed by the Pharisees (Matthew 23:23)

Quiz 34

1. fruit of the spirit (Galatians 5:22–23)

2. Cain (Genesis 4:2–15)

3. Solomon (1 Kings 11:1–3; 1 Kings 4:32)

4. fathers and sons (Genesis 5:28–29; 1 Samuel 17:17; Genesis 22:1–2)

5. naked people (Genesis 2:25; Job 1:21; Mark 14:51–52)

6. rivers (2 Kings 5:12; Genesis 15:18)

7. multiple languages (John 19:19–20; Genesis 11:5–9; Acts 2:1–11)

8. Philistines (Judges 14:1–3; Genesis 26:8; 1 Samuel 17:4–8)

9. Nicodemus (John 3:1–7)

10. the prophet Nahum (Nahum 1:1–14)

Quiz 35

1. people Jesus blessed in His beatitudes (Matthew 5:1–10)

2. Joseph (Genesis 37:2–4)

3. Adam and Eve after the fall (Genesis 3:17–24)

4. Jesus' baptism (Mark 1:9–11)

5. twins (Genesis 38:27–30; Genesis 25:24–26; Song of Solomon 4:5)

6. things that surround God's throne in heaven (Revelation 4:1–8)

7. Enoch (Genesis 5:21–24)

8. Abigail (1 Samuel 25:2–42)

9. Ahab (1 Kings 16:29–31)

10. kings of Babylon (2 Kings 25:27; Ezra 5:13; 2 Chronicles 36:6)

Quiz 36

1. miracles of Jesus (Mark 8:22–25; John 11:38–44; Mark 6:45–50)

2. twelve (Deuteronomy 1:22–23; Mark 6:42–44; Luke 2:41–49)

3. titles of Jesus Christ (Matthew 8:20; Matthew 1:1; Matthew 8:29–31)

4. Joseph (Genesis 37:12–36)

5. people who were beaten (Exodus 5:14; 2 Corinthians 11:25; Matthew 27:27–30)

6. beds (Luke 5:17–19; Exodus 8:1–3; Hebrews 13:4)

7. beheadings (Revelation 20:4; Matthew 14:6–10; 1 Samuel 17:51)

8. quotations from the book of Hebrews (Hebrews 2:3; Hebrews 4:9; Hebrews 10:25)

9. units of liquid measurement (Ezekiel 45:14)

10. people the apostle Paul greeted in his epistles (Romans 16:8; Colossians 4:15; Romans 16:7)

Quiz 37

1. Israel (Genesis 49:28; Genesis 32:28; Psalm 135:4)

2. the story of the good Samaritan (Luke 10:25–37)

3. Jerusalem (Matthew 23:37; Psalm 122:6; Nehemiah 11:1)

4. fathers and sons (Joshua 1:1; Jonah 1:1; Mark 1:1)

5. people who saw Jesus after His resurrection (Luke 24:13–18; John 20:26–29; 1 Corinthians 15:3–6)

6. quotations from the book of Romans (Romans 3:23; Romans 1:16; Romans 6:23)

7. high priests (John 18:22–24; 2 Kings 23:4–9; Hebrews 4:14–16)

8. tribute, or taxes (Mark 12:13–17; Matthew 17:24–27; Luke 2:1–5)

9. kings of Israel (1 Kings 16:16; 1 Kings 22:39–40; 2 Kings 10:35–36)

10. groaning (Exodus 2:23–24; Romans 8:19–22; Romans 8:26)

Quiz 38

1. wise men (Matthew 2:1–11)

2. names of God (Psalm 71:22; James 1:17; Exodus 3:14)

3. Pontius Pilate (Luke 3:1; Luke 23:16–25)

4. the first three days of creation (Genesis 1:1–13)

5. Saul's (Paul's) conversion experience (Acts 9:1–19)

6. Cana of Galilee (John 4:46–54; John 21:2; John 2:1–11)

7. green things (Song of Solomon 1:16; Genesis 1:30–31; Psalm 23:2)

8. hail (Exodus 9:13–18; Revelation 16:17–21; John 19:1–3)

9. tithes (Matthew 23:23; Genesis 14:18–20; Malachi 3:10)

10. sufferings of the faithful (Hebrews 11:36–38)

Quiz 39

1. men named Judas (Luke 6:13–16; Matthew 13:55; Matthew 10:4)

2. titles of Jesus Christ (1 Peter 5:1–4; John 1:29; Revelation 5:5)

3. red things (Genesis 25:25; Isaiah 1:18; Exodus 14:21–15:4)

4. manna (Exodus 16:1–15)

5. Rachel (Genesis 46:19; Genesis 29:28; Genesis 30:8–9)

6. people who ran (Luke 15:11–20; John 20:1–4; Acts 8:26–30)

7. Lot (Genesis 13:11; Genesis 19:1; Genesis 19:23)

8. judges of Israel (Judges 3:9–10; Judges 10:3; Judges 12:11)

9. words connected with "Jehovah" (Exodus 17:15; Judges 6:24; Genesis 22:14)

10. things God commanded people to write (Habakkuk 2:2; Revelation 1:9–11; Exodus 17:8–14)

Quiz 40

1. Bethlehem (Micah 5:2; Luke 2:1–7; Matthew 2:1)

2. the fall of Jericho (Joshua 5:13–6:5)

3. things people shouted at Jesus (John 12:13; Matthew 27:29; Luke 23:21)

4. Jesus' parable of the talents (Matthew 25:14–30)

5. Rebekah (Genesis 22:23; Genesis 24:67; Genesis 25:21–26)

6. ravens (Song of Solomon 5:10–11; 1 Kings 17:1–4; Genesis 8:6–7)

7. the handwriting on the wall (Daniel 5:1–25)

8. types of spirits (Mark 6:7; 1 Timothy 4:1; Hebrews 1:14)

9. minor characters in the story of Esther (Esther 2:21; Esther 6:13; Esther 4:5)

10. kings of Persia (Ezra 1:1; Ezra 4:5; Ezra 7:1)

Quiz 41

1. the birth of Jesus (Matthew 2:2; Luke 2:4; Luke 2:7)

2. parables of Jesus (Luke 18:9–14; Luke 16:19–31; Luke 15:3–7)

3. John the Baptist (Matthew 3:6; Matthew 3:7; Luke 3:16)

4. Jacob and Esau (Genesis 25:29–34)

5. peace (Galatians 5:22–23; John 14:27; Psalm 122:6)

6. people in prison (Genesis 39:1–20; Judges 16:20–21; Acts 16:12–29)

7. quotations from the book of Proverbs (Proverbs 6:6; Proverbs 15:1; Proverbs 3:5)

8. the golden calf (Exodus 32:2–20)

9. the prophet Isaiah (Isaiah 6:1; Isaiah 8:3; Isaiah 1:1)

10. colors of the four horses of Revelation (Revelation 6:1–8)

Quiz 42

1. David (1 Samuel 16:23; 1 Chronicles 16:7; 1 Samuel 17:50)

2. the Ten Commandments (Exodus 20:1–17)

3. Leah (Genesis 29:21–25; Genesis 29:32–33; Genesis 30:8–9)

4. quotations from the book of Proverbs (Proverbs 20:1; Proverbs 27:5; Proverbs 10:1)

5. things Jesus said not to worry about (Matthew 6:31–32)

6. foxes (Matthew 8:20; Judges 15:3–5; Luke 13:31–32)

7. the gospel (Romans 1:16; Mark 16:15; Ephesians 6:19)

8. handmaids or maidservants (Genesis 25:12; Genesis 35:25; Luke 1:38)

9. hard things (1 Kings 10:1; 2 Peter 3:15–16; Exodus 10:20)

10. things the Lord hates (Proverbs 6:16–19)

Quiz 43

1. "I am" statements of Jesus (Revelation 1:17–18; John 9:1–5; John 14:6)

2. Samson (Judges 16:17–20)

3. arguments Jesus used to battle Satan's temptation (Luke 4:1–13)

4. characters in the book of Daniel (Daniel 2:14; Daniel 5:30–31; Daniel 1:7)

5. Golgotha (Mark 15:22–23; John 19:16–18)

6. the armor of God (Ephesians 6:13–17)

7. cedar (2 Samuel 7:1–5; Job 40:15–17; Psalm 92:12)

8. events in the book of Matthew (Matthew 2:1–12; Matthew 2:13–18; Matthew 28:1–6)

9. problems in the church at Corinth (1 Corinthians 1:10–12; 1 Corinthians 6:1–6; 1 Corinthians 5:1)

10. Ephesus (Ephesians 1:1; Acts 19:23–41; Revelation 2:1–7)

Quiz 44

1. the apostle Peter (Matthew 14:28–29; John 21:15–17; 1 Peter 1:1–2)

2. miracles of Jesus (John 2:1–11; Matthew 8:23–27; Luke 17:11–19)

3. the Transfiguration (Luke 9:28–36)

4. Samson (Judges 13:2–3; Judges 16:17; Judges 16:23–30)

5. Moses (Exodus 3:1; Exodus 5:1; Numbers 27:18)

6. spies in Canaan (Numbers 13:1–25)

7. events in the book of John (John 2:1–11; John 3:1–7; John 11:1–44)

8. judgments of Revelation (Revelation 6:1–14; Revelation 8:6–9:21; Revelation 16:1)

9. the apostle Paul's journey to Rome (Acts 27:1–44)

10. Job's friends and "comforters" (Job 2:11)

Quiz 45

1. faith (Hebrews 11:1; James 2:20; Hebrews 10:38)

2. Jesus' death (Luke 23:44–47)

3. the woman at the well (John 4:1–26)

4. the family line of Jesus (Luke 3:23–24)

5. meekness (Galatians 5:22–23; Numbers 12:3; Matthew 5:5)

6. events in the book of Acts (Acts 1:1–11; Acts 2:1–4; Acts 5:1–11)

7. signs of Christ's coming (Matthew 24:3–14)

8. women who supported Jesus' ministry (Luke 8:1–3)

9. wives of King David (1 Chronicles 3:1–4)

10. things the Lord hates (Proverbs 6:16–19)

Quiz 46

1. man (Genesis 1:26–28)

2. fish (John 21:12–13; John 21:11; Jonah 1:17)

3. mountains (1 Kings 18:19; Deuteronomy 3:8; Psalm 74:2)

4. grace (Genesis 6:8; 2 Corinthians 12:9; Hebrews 4:16)

5. Jesus' triumphal entry into Jerusalem (Matthew 21:1–11)

6. godliness (1 Timothy 3:16; 1 Timothy 4:8; 1 Timothy 6:6)

7. teeth (Jeremiah 31:29; Exodus 21:24; Matthew 13:42)

8. events in the book of Revelation (Revelation 11:1–12; Revelation 20:1–2; Revelation 21:3–4)

9. rivers (Deuteronomy 3:16; Daniel 8:2; Judges 5:21)

10. Crete (Titus 1:12; Acts 27:12; Titus 1:5)

Quiz 47

1. Passover (Exodus 12:1–11)

2. Abram, or Abraham (Genesis 14:11–16; Genesis 18:13–14; Genesis 17:3–5)

3. plagues on Egypt (Exodus 7:14–19; Exodus 8:16–17; Exodus 9:8–12)

4. Jesus' comments to people who said they wanted to follow Him (Matthew 8:20; Matthew 8:22; Luke 9:62)

5. cutting hair (Acts 18:18; 2 Samuel 14:25–26; Judges 16:18–22)

6. wine (1 Timothy 5:23; Numbers 6:2–3; Ephesians 5:18)

7. events in the book of Luke (Luke 1:57–66; Luke 2:8–20; Luke 2:41–52)

8. Caleb (Numbers 13:6; Joshua 14:13; Numbers 13:26–30)

9. mountains (Numbers 33:37; Judges 4:14; 2 Chronicles 3:1)

10. Dorcas (Acts 9:36–41)

Quiz 48

1. Moses (Exodus 1:15–2:10; Exodus 2:11–15; Deuteronomy 34:1–5)

2. Elisabeth (Luke 1:5; Luke 1:57–60; Luke 1:34–37)

3. enemies (Esther 3:10; Matthew 5:44; Mark 12:36)

4. fire (Exodus 13:21–22; Revelation 20:14–15; 1 Kings 18:22–24)

5. fingers (John 20:26–27; Daniel 5:1–6; 1 Chronicles 20:6–7)

6. firstborn sons (Genesis 46:8; Genesis 27:19–20; Exodus 12:29–30)

7. swords (Ephesians 6:17; John 18:10; Isaiah 2:4)

8. Mary's song, also known as the Magnificat (Luke 1:46–55)

9. Matthias (Acts 1:18–26)

10. quotations from the book of 1 John (1 John 3:1; 1 John 4:8; 1 John 4:19)

Quiz 49

1. Peter's denial of Jesus (Matthew 26:69–75)

2. Abraham and Isaac (Genesis 22:1–13)

3. feet (Isaiah 52:7; Luke 7:36–38; Psalm 119:105)

4. the number eight (1 Samuel 17:12; 2 Kings 22:1; 1 Peter 3:20)

5. Jesus' death (Matthew 27:50–53)

6. fathers' relationships to their children (Ephesians 6:4)

7. places in the book of Revelation (Revelation 20:7–8; Revelation 17:5; Revelation 16:16)

8. nicknames (Judges 6:32; Mark 3:17; Acts 4:36)

9. people who won't inherit the kingdom of God (1 Corinthians 6:9–10)

10. Jael (Judges 4:17–21)

Quiz 50

1. God (1 Timothy 1:17)

2. Jesus' "Great Commission" (Matthew 28:18–20)

3. image (Exodus 20:4; Genesis 1:26; Colossians 1:15)

4. the Roman soldiers' mocking of Jesus (Matthew 27:27–31)

5. virgins (Judges 11:30–40; Luke 1:26–27; Matthew 25:1)

6. the church (Philippians 3:6; Ephesians 5:23; Matthew 16:18)

7. blood (Genesis 4:9–10; Luke 8:43–48; Leviticus 8:19)

8. Herodias (Mark 6:17–28)

9. things to remember (Luke 17:32; Colossians 4:18; Exodus 20:8)

10. bitter things (Exodus 12:8; Luke 22:61–62; Exodus 15:22–24)

Quiz 51

1. types of money (Mark 12:42; Luke 12:6; Matthew 22:19)

2. men named James (Matthew 13:55; Matthew 10:3; Matthew 10:2)

3. the resurrection of Jesus (John 20:1–9)

4. Nazareth (Mark 1:9; John 1:46; Matthew 2:19–23)

5. crowns (1 Corinthians 9:25; John 19:5; Revelation 4:10–11)

6. the ark of the testimony (Exodus 25:10–22)

7. valleys (Joshua 7:26; Joshua 18:16; Psalm 23:4)

8. boils (Exodus 9:8–9; 2 Kings 20:1–7; Job 2:7–8)

9. blasphemy (Revelation 17:3; Matthew 26:57–66; Matthew 12:31)

10. "blessed" people (Psalm 1:1; Psalm 32:1; Psalm 33:12)

Quiz 52

1. measurements of length (Exodus 28:16; Exodus 25:10; Revelation 21:16)

2. "I am" statements of Jesus (John 8:23; John 15:1; Revelation 1:8)

3. neighbors (Exodus 20:17; Matthew 19:19; Luke 10:25–37)

4. men named Jeremiah (Nehemiah 12:1; 1 Chronicles 12:1–4; Jeremiah 13:17)

5. vows (Acts 18:18; Judges 11:30–39; 1 Samuel 1:10–11)

6. men named Daniel (1 Chronicles 3:1; Nehemiah 10:1–6; Daniel 6:16)

7. events in the book of Acts (Acts 7:54–60; Acts 9:1–16; Acts 12:1–11)

8. "blessed" people (Luke 12:37; Psalm 112:1; James 1:12)

9. places in the Bible (Genesis 41:45; Genesis 11:28; Job 1:1)

10. hypocrites (Luke 6:42; Matthew 6:16; Matthew 23:29)